In Control

*A Book of Games to Teach
Children Self-Control Skills*

By Lawrence E. Shapiro, Ph.D.

Childswork/Childsplay
Plainview, New York

In Control
A Book of Games to Teach Children Self-Control Skills

By Lawrence E. Shapiro, Ph.D.

Childswork/Childsplay publishes products for mental heath professionals, teachers and parents who wish to help children with their developmental, social and emotional growth. For questions, comments, or to request a free catalog describing hundreds of games, toys, books, and other counseling tools, call 1-800-962-1141.

© 1995 Childswork/Childsplay, LLC
A Guidance Channel Company
135 Dupont Street
Plainview, NY 11803

ISBN 1-882732-40-5

ABOUT THIS BOOK

In Control is a book of six games designed to help children learn self-control skills. The book comes with a single game board, bound in the center of the book. You may wish to leave the board in the book, or remove it and tape the the two sides together. Laminating the board and mounting it on heavy cardboard or foamcore will make it more durable.

Attached to your book you will find the following game pieces:

> 1 regular 6-sided die
> 1 30-sided die
> 50 chips
> 6 pawns
> 1 minute timer

Also bound in the book are:
> **Feelings Faces** Cards (used in Game 1)
> **In Control** Cards (used in Game 2)
> **I.O.U.** Cards (used in Game 4)

Each game comes with three sets of numbered questions, statements, or situations, which are selected by rolling the 30-sided die included with your book. The number the die lands on is the numbered item that is read. To have the lists available while you play the game, we recommend that you make a copy of each list, or remove them from the book.

You will also note that in each list, we have left numbers 26-30 for you to fill in. This can be done by the adult who is playing or supervising the game, or by the children themselves. Therapeutic games work best when they are individualized to the unique circumstances and concerns of the children who are playing them, and writing your own questions is the best way to individualize the game.

TABLE OF CONTENTS

INTRODUCTION

How Children Learn Self-Control

Teaching Self-Control

Problems in self-control are among the major concerns of educators and mental health professionals. When children are overly aggressive, impulsive, inattentive, or undisciplined, we assume that they do not have the motivation or perhaps the ability to meet our behavioral expectations.

Many studies have pointed to differences between children who are compliant and interested in following adult rules and those with problems in self-control. Children with behavioral problems related to self-control typically do not use age-appropriate cognitive processes to adapt to and affect their environment, including such cognitive skills as problem solving, planning ahead, organizing, decision making and so on. These children may also have problems understanding and expressing their own emotions, picking up on the emotional cues of others, and incorporating adult rules and expectations into their behavioral repertoire.

The assumptions of this book are that many of the skills involved in developing self-control can be taught, and that games are one of the most effective techniques to teach these psychological skills.

The Principles of Therapeutic Games

For more than 25 years, therapeutic games have been used to help children communicate and understand their problems while developing new cognitive and behavioral skills. Games are uniquely suited to helping children with problems in self-control for a variety of reasons. First, the rules of the game provide a structure which makes the behavioral expectations for children both clear and predictable. Second, winning chips in the game is motivating for children even if they are resistant to playing a psychological game. With very resistant children, the adult can let the players cash in their chips for small prizes or privileges, which will further their motivation to play. The psychological game combines a variety of therapeutic principles. It simultaneously helps children communicate about problems, while it teaches them specific cognitive and behavioral skills. The child with problems in self-control will also learn important social skills while playing the game, including taking turns, listening to others, following rules, and so on.

Games are also among the most highly adaptable of all psychological strategies. The rules can be modified to suit the needs of the individual child or group of children. The cards can be changed or supplemented. And, perhaps most importantly, the game can be played in a wide variety of settings with nearly any adult who is willing to learn and practice the most basic psychological principles of working with children.

The Multimodal Approach

The six games included in this book represent a multimodal approach to helping children. This approach assumes that the best way to help children with their problems is to look at them from not one, but several different points of view. The self-control games included in this book represent six important modalities that can be used in helping children learn self-control skills: affect, behavior, cognition, developmental, educational, and social. These modalities are easy to remember, because they represent the ABCDE'S approach to helping children.

The Affective Modality

You Hurt My Feelings! is specifically designed to help children understand how their behavior affects others. Children with problems in self-control typically do not see themselves as being difficult and they view the adults who punish them as being unfair. As children learn to understand how their behavior makes other people feel, they will be presumably become better at expressing their own feelings and acting in ways that are more socially appropriate. Although researchers tell us that children do not develop true empathy until the ages of 12-14, when they can truly see another person's point of view, children as young as five can learn to act in ways which consider the needs and differences of others and bring them the approval of adults and their peers.

The Behavioral Modality

I'm **In Control!** deals with the issues of behavioral impulsivity. This game is designed to help children look ahead at possible consequences to their behavior, avoid people or situations that might lead to behavior problems, and develop a strategy as well as a backup plan to deal with provocation. This game assumes that one of the best ways to prevent behavioral problems is to help children learn to avoid situations and people that might cause them to act inappropriately. This includes learning to deal with other children who might tease or provoke them, a common reason why school-age children become angry and aggressive.

The Cognitive Modality

Teaching children to talk to themselves is one of the more common ways to teach children self-control skills. We know that children who are reflective rather than impulsive talk to themselves as a way of controlling their behavior. Their internal dialogue is referred to as self-guiding or self-regulating speech. The assumptions behind this game are that thoughts are like behaviors in that they can be learned by practice and reinforcement, and therefore children with problems in self-control can inhibit their impulsivity by learning to talk to themselves. The metaphor behind **Self-Coaching** is that of an athlete learning a sport. Children are asked to coach themselves by learning to say encouraging things to themselves and turn negative statements into positive ones.

The Developmental Modality

The developmental modality refers to any set of behaviors or abilities that develop as the child ages. More than others their age, children with problems in self-control tend to have deficits in their organizational skills, particularly in the area of time. Adults may interpret their difficulties (not being in the right place at the right time with the right attitude) as a sign of defiance, but these problems could also be attributed to their lack of specific organizational abilities. **Right on Time!** was designed to help children learn the importance of making a schedule and keeping to it.

The Educational Modality

Helping Others was designed to address the issues of teaching children good values. Even if children have self-control problems, when they are good-hearted and express concern for others, they are well liked by their teachers and peers. Many studies have suggested that being well liked is one of the most important factors in school and personal success. While some children seem to be naturally concerned about others, many other children need to be taught about the importance of helping others and being selfless. Taking the time to teach these values may be one of the most important ways an adult can help a child with problems in self-control.

The Social Modality

Virtually every child who has problems with self-control has concomitant social problems. Because of the difficulties these children have in communicating and controlling their feelings and behaviors, they often suffer from peer rejection and isolation. Not only does this lower their self-esteem, but it also prevents these children from experiencing the richness of childhood friendships which will form the basis of their future relationships. **Can I Play, Too?** concentrates on three specific social skills: social entry, making friends, and group cooperation.

Ideally, the games will be selected to match the needs as well as the strengths of an individual child. If the adult is not sure which game to begin with, it might be useful to explain the six different games to the child and let him/her help in making the choice. Alternatively, all six games could be played over a period of time, using the games as both a means of learning more about a child's self-control problems while simultaneously treating them. Since one of the best ways to treat children with self-control problems is through a counseling group, the games could also be used as a vehicle for stimulating discussion and rehearsing skills in a Self-Control Club.

There is really no wrong way to use the games in this book, as long as the adult supervising the games follows some basic rules:

1. Be compassionate, even if the child is difficult and defiant. The relationship you have with the child is one of the most powerful therapeutic variables.

2. Keep to the structure of the game. Once a game has started, don't let children change the rules or cheat. You can modify rules in a later game if it is psychologically appropriate to do so.

3. Remember the psychological principles behind each game. Emphasize the principles behind each modality when you are playing the game.

4. Use the games as part of a complete treatment plan. The games should be used as part of an overall strategy to help the child, which might include classroom intervention, parent counseling or training, or other psychological strategies.

5. Above all...HAVE FUN! Remember, the main motivating element of a game is that it is fun to play.

YOU HURT MY FEELINGS!

Introduction:
Children with problems in self-control typically have problems both in expressing their feelings in appropriate ways and in understanding and empathizing with the feeling of others. As they begin to understand how their behavior affects others, they become more sensitized to both the internal cues that accompany their emotions and the external cues that indicate the emotions of others. As children become less egocentric, they are in turn more motivated to develop the self-control skills which will win them social approval.

Objectives:

- To help children understand how their behaviors can affect other people

- To help children understand what to do when they have done something that upsets someone else

- To help children understand the best ways to express their feelings so that they are understood by others

What You Will Need:
1 pawn for each player
1 regular 6-sided die
1 30-sided die
Chips

Make copies of the following pages or remove them from the book:
Other People's Feelings Questions (p. 7)
I'm Sorry Questions (p. 9)
Saying What You Feel and Want Questions (p. 13)
Feelings Faces Cards (pp. 17 and 19). Make one copy of each of these pages for each player, and have them cut out the cards.

How to Play:

This game can be played by two to six players. The youngest player goes first and play proceeds in a clockwise direction. Each person should have a "deck" of the 16 **Feelings Faces** cards. Fewer feelings can be used with younger children, or more feelings can be added to the page for older children (e.g. anxious, irritable, upset, joyful, etc.). It is important that each child have a deck of exactly the same feelings. Each player rolls the 6-sided die and moves his/her pawn the corresponding number of squares. If the player lands on a:

He/she must roll the 30-sided die to choose an **Other People's Feelings** question and then read the question to the player on the right. That player then makes a face that corresponds to his/her feelings about the question, selects the corresponding **Feelings Faces** card from his/her deck, and places it face down. The original player must then try to choose the matching **Feelings Faces** card from his/her deck and place it face up on the table. If the two **Feelings Faces** cards match, the first player gets a chip.

He/she must roll the 30-sided die to choose an **I'm Sorry** question. The player gets one chip for answering the question thoughtfully.

He/she must roll the 30-sided die to choose a **Saying What You Feel and Want** situation. The player gets one chip for using an "I-Statement" in response.

Each list of questions includes five blank numbers for you to fill in by yourself or with the child. If you do not wish to add numbers 26 through 30, when these numbers come up on the die, the player should roll again.

Play proceeds until the first player lands back at the START. The player with the most chips at the end of the game is the winner.

Other People's Feelings

WHEN THE FIRST STAR IS LANDED ON, READ THE FOLLOWING TO THE PLAYERS:

It is important to understand how other people feel. Roll the 30-sided die to choose a question. Then read it to the player on your right. He/she must make a face that expresses his/her feeling about that question, and then place the appropriate Feelings Faces card face down. Try to guess the feeling. Then, from your own deck, put out the card you think is correct. If the cards match, you get a chip. If they don't match, the other player should explain his/her feeling to you.

Variation: If players know each other well, they don't have to make a face in answer to a question; they can just put out a card. The other players should be able to predict their feelings to each question without a visual cue.

★1. How do you feel when you are called on in class?

★2. What was your first feeling when you got up this morning?

★3. How did you feel when you got your last test back?

★4. How did you feel the last time you had a discussion with your father?

★5. How did you feel on the first day of school?

★6. How did you feel the last time you talked to your best friend?

★7. How did you feel when you got on the bus this morning?

★8. How did you feel when you went to bed last night?

★9. How did you feel the last time your mother scolded you?

★10. How did you feel the last time you saw your grandfather?

★11. How do you feel at recess?

★12. How do you feel at your team's practices?

★13. How do you feel when your brother comes home from school?

★14. How did you feel when studying for your last test?

★15. How do you feel when you give reports in front of the class?

★16. How would you feel if someone in your class kissed you?

★17. How do you feel when you make someone else laugh?

★18. How do you feel when your mom and dad fight?

★19. How did you feel when you last went to your friend's house to play?

★20. How do you feel when your grandmother invites you to her house?

★21. How do you feel when your mom asks you to help with the chores?

★22. How do you feel when someone tells a joke?

★23. How do you feel at the playground near your house?

★24. How do you feel when you get invited to a party?

★25. How did you feel the last time you answered a question wrong in class?

★26. _____

★27. _____

★28. _____

★29. _____

★30. _____

●

I'm Sorry

WHEN THE FIRST CIRCLE IS LANDED ON, READ THE FOLLOWING TO THE PLAYERS:

When you do something to upset someone else, the first thing you should do is to say you are sorry. But saying you're sorry is not really enough. What can you do to show that you are really sorry?

●1.   You forgot to invite Mary to your party even though she is your close friend. You heard from another friend that she was crying just before school started. What can you do to make things right again?

●2.   You were banging your silverware at the table, even though your mother said that she had a splitting headache. Then she screamed at you to stop! What can you do to make things right again?

●3.   You forgot to make a card for your grandmother's birthday. She said that her feelings were hurt. What can you do to make things right again?

●4.   You told someone that the new boy in school smelled bad. You know that he overheard you. What can you do to make things right again?

●5.   You took money from your father's dresser drawer and he caught you. He said he wasn't going to punish you, but he was disappointed in you. What can you do to make things right again?

●6.   Yesterday you told your best friend that you'd help her study for today's spelling test, but you forgot and played video games instead. Now she's upset because she's afraid she'll fail the test. What can you do to make things right again?

●7.   When your mom came home, she found you playing with a friend instead of setting the table, even though she's repeatedly asked you to help out more around the house. What can you do to make things right again?

●8.   A friend dared you to take a candy bar from the corner store. You did – and didn't get caught – but now you feel badly about it. What can you do to make things right again?

●9.   Your aunt came to visit and gave you a big wet kiss when she arrived. You wiped it off your cheek and ran upstairs to your room, making sure everyone knew how gross you thought it was. Now your mom's telling you that your aunt is upset. What can you do to make things right again?

●10   The neighbors just asked you to baby-sit because their sitter canceled at the last minute. You had plans to just watch TV all evening and said you couldn't do it. Now your neighbors are missing the wife's company party and they're really disappointed. What can you do to make things right again?

●11.   You volunteered to stay after school and help clean the classroom, but you just found out that your friends are playing soccer in the park. In all the excitement, you go with them. The next day, the teacher scolds you for not helping him. What can you do to make things right again?

●12.   You're having a hard time in math and got really fed up last night studying for today's quiz. Since you sit behind the smartest kid in class, you find yourself looking over her shoulder to copy an answer. Just then, the teacher sees you copying. What can you do to make things right again?

●13.   You promised your dad that if you got a puppy, you'd take care of it. Last night though, you forgot to lock the gate and your puppy ran away. What can you do to make things right again?

●14.   You made fun of your brother when he came home with braces on his teeth; then, you saw him crying in his room. What can you do to make things right again?

●15.   At the dinner table, you and your sister always joke around with each other and sometimes get kind of rowdy. Last night, you started laughing so hard that you accidentally knocked over your glass of milk and it spilled on the rug. What can you do to make things right again?

●16.   Some bigger kids were pushing around a friend of yours at recess, so you went over and started picking on them. Soon, a teacher came over to break it up and you got in trouble. What can you do to make things right again?

●17. You usually visit your grandfather every Monday, but this week you forgot. Now he's sad because he missed playing cards with you. What can you do to make things right again?

●18. You were supposed to walk your little sister home from school, but your friends talked you into going to the arcade right after last period. When you get home, your mom is furious with you. What can you do to make things right again?

●19. Your best friend decides he want to try out for chorus. You think that's lame and call him a sissy. Tonight when you call him, his mom tells you he doesn't want to talk to you. What can you do to make things right again?

●20. You told your mom you'd stop at the store and get milk for her on your way home from visiting your friend, but there was a baseball game in the park that totally distracted you. Your mom was a little upset when you arrived without the milk. What can you do to make things right again?

●21. As a joke, you hid your little sister's favorite doll and now she's crying to your mom that she can't find it anywhere. What can you do to make things right again?

●22. You got mad at your coach for yelling at you before the softball game, so you decided not to field very well. In the last inning, you missed a pop fly and lost the game for your team and everybody got mad at you. What can you do to make things right again?

●23. You were making fun of the teacher when she walked in the classroom and heard you. She said you hurt her feelings. What can you do to make things right again?

●24. Your dad asked you not to play with his new stereo unless he was around to help you. But you had friends over and wanted to play a cool new CD for them. A CD got stuck in the player and when your dad came home, he was pretty mad. What can you do to make things right again?

●25. Everyone knows that you get the back seat on the school bus, everyone except the new kid who is sitting there when you get on this morning. You get angry and tell him it's your seat and he has to get out, which causes a fight and you both get detention. What can you do to make things right again?

●26. _____

●27. _____

●28. _____

●29. _____

●30. _____

Saying What You Feel and Want

WHEN THE FIRST DIAMOND IS LANDED ON, READ THE FOLLOWING TO THE PLAYERS:

Communicating feelings is a skill that has to be learned. Good communication always begins with YOU! The easiest way to practice good communication is through the use of "I-Statements." When you have strong feelings about something, you can best make them known by filling in the blanks in the sentence below. Respond to each question by communicating with "I-Statements" using the formula below. (Example: "I feel happy when you play a game with me because it shows me that you like me and I want to play more often!")

I feel _____

when you _____

because _____

and I want _____.

◆1.   Pretend the player on your right is your best friend. He just said you were stupid because you didn't want to play with him. Tell him how you feel using an "I-Statement."

◆2.   Pretend the player on your right is your dad. He said that he is too busy to take you bowling, even though he promised. Tell him how you feel using an "I-Statement."

◆3.   Pretend the player on your right is your brother. He just told your parents that you got a "D" on your spelling test, before you had a chance to tell them. Tell him how you feel using an "I-Statement."

◆4. Pretend the player on your right is your teacher. She embarrassed you in front of the class, by saying that you are absent-minded because you often forget to hand in your homework. Tell her how you feel after class, using an "I-Statement."

◆5. Pretend the player on your right is an older kid who makes fun of you because you wear glasses. Tell him how you feel using an "I-Statement."

◆6. Pretend the person on your right is your older sister. She just told a group of her friends what a baby you are because you're afraid of the dark. Tell her how you feel using an "I-Statement."

◆7. Pretend the person on your right is your grandmother. She just came to visit and brought your brother a present, but didn't bring one for you. Tell her how you feel using an "I-Statement."

◆8. Pretend the person on your right is your best friend. He/she just said in front of the class that you aren't allowed to go to the party on Friday. Tell him/her how you feel using an "I-Statement."

◆9. Pretend the person on your right is your coach. He/she benched you during the game for getting into a fight that you didn't even start. Tell him/her how you feel using an "I-Statement."

◆10. Pretend the person on your right is your dad. Every day he comes home, and all he wants to do is drink a beer and watch TV. Why can't he play with you for a change? Tell him how you feel using an "I-Statement."

◆11. Pretend the person on your right is your neighbor. She always yells at you if you walk on her side of the yard when you're playing out back, and tells your parents you always disturb her. Tell her how you feel using an "I-Statement."

◆12. Pretend the person on your right is your mom. Whenever you bring home anything lower than an "A" from school – even a "B" – she starts to lecture you about working harder. Tell her how you feel using an "I-Statement."

◆13. Pretend the person on your right is your classmate. He always tells you that his parents let him do whatever he wants, and that your parents don't love you as much because they make you do your homework and make you walk to school. Tell him how you feel using an "I-Statement."

◆14. Pretend the person on your right is your aunt. She tells you that your parents always fight when you're not around, and sometimes they even hit each other. Tell her how you feel using an "I-Statement."

◆15. Pretend the person on your right is your bus driver. When kids get loud on the bus after school, he yells back and swears at them. Everybody is afraid of him, including you. Tell him how you feel using an "I-Statement."

◆16. Pretend the person on your right is your uncle. Every time he comes to visit, he seems to get you alone in a room and starts to touch you in ways you don't want to be touched. Tell him how you feel using an "I-Statement."

◆17. Pretend the person on your right is your gym teacher. You can't run as fast as everyone else, so when you lag behind running laps, the teacher makes fun of you for being slow. Tell him how you feel using an "I-Statement."

◆18. Pretend the person on your right is your older brother. He plays soccer with his friends every day after school and never asks if you want to come along. Tell him how you feel using an "I-Statement."

◆19. Pretend the person on your right is an older kid at school. Every time you go out to recess, he always picks on you, but nobody else. You've never done anything to him. Tell him how you feel using an "I-Statement."

◆20. Pretend the person on your right is your teacher. He just announced everyone's grades out loud and you got a "D." You feel really embarrassed. Tell him how you feel using an "I-Statement."

◆21. Pretend that the person on your right is your dad. He just yelled at you for forgetting to clean your room, even though he knows you were helping your neighbor pick up her groceries this morning. Tell him how you feel using an "I-Statement."

◆22. Pretend the person on your right is your principal. She just gave you detention for being late to school for the fifth time this month. But your parents work and you have to get all your younger brothers and sisters ready for school yourself. Tell her how you feel using an "I-Statement."

◆23. Pretend the person on your right is your classmate. You just found out that you're the only person who's not invited to his birthday party. Tell him how you feel using an "I-Statement."

◆24. Pretend the person on your right is your mom. She just yelled at you for screaming in the house after she asked you to be quiet, but your older brother was chasing you around and tickling you. Tell her how you feel using an "I-Statement."

◆25. Pretend the person on your right is your baby-sitter. She starts to boss you around as soon as your parents walk out the door, and tries to act like she's your mom. You think she's mean. Tell her how you feel using an "I-Statement."

◆26. _____

◆27. _____

◆28. _____

◆29. _____

◆30. _____

FEELINGS FACES

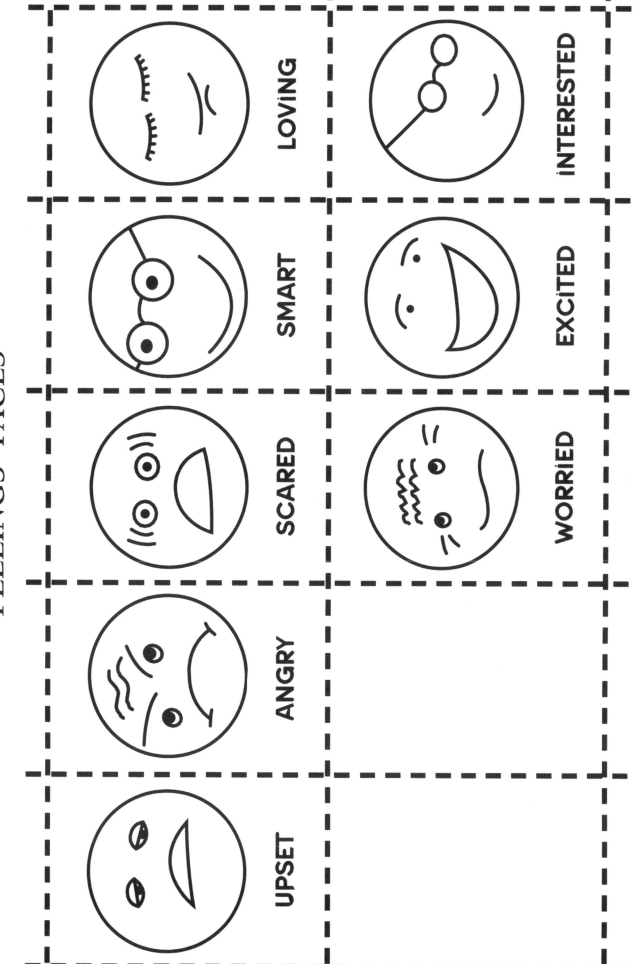

LOVING

INTERESTED

SMART

EXCITED

SCARED

WORRIED

ANGRY

UPSET

FEELINGS FACES

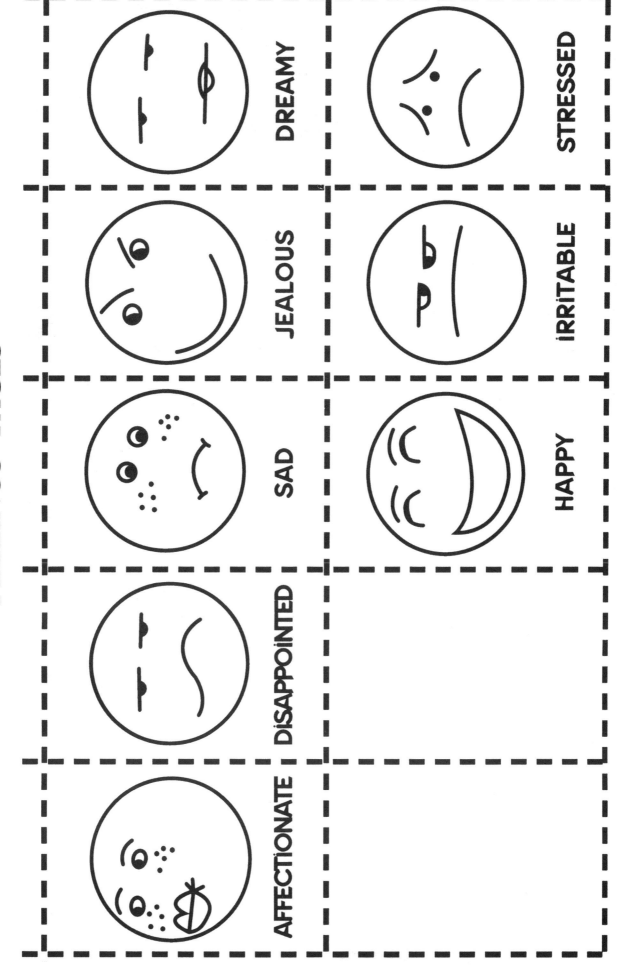

Game #2

I'M IN CONTROL!

Introduction:
There are many components to behavioral impulsivity, and for the most part, this behavior is not an easy one to change. Studies have shown that even infants can be categorized as being either reflective or impulsive, and this trait seems to be fairly stable throughout childhood. Nevertheless, even the most impulsive child must learn to control this trait as he/she begins school and must meet the ever-increasing expectations for control in social situations. This game is designed to help children rehearse patience and frustration tolerance, and to recognize situations where these qualities are important.

Objectives:
- To help children learn the importance of looking ahead at possible consequences
- To help children avoid people or situations that might lead to behavioral problems
- To help children develop a strategy and a backup plan to deal with provocation

What You Will Need:
    1 pawn for each player
    1 regular 6-sided die
    1 30-sided die
    Minute timer
    Chips
    Drawing paper (not included)
    6 **In Control** Cards

Make copies of the following pages or remove them from the book:
    Look Ahead! Situations (p. 23)
    You Can't Make Me Do It! Situations (p. 26)
    Keep It Steady (p. 28)
    In Control Cards (p. 29)

How to Play:

This game can be played by two to six players. The youngest player goes first and play proceeds in a clockwise direction. Each player rolls the die and moves his/her pawn the corresponding number of squares. If the player lands on a:

He/she must respond to a **Look Ahead!** situation (p. 23). The first time a star is landed on, read the statement at the top of the page. Then the player should throw the 30-sided die to choose the situation. The player then has one minute (using the timer) to draw a picture of what will happen next. If he/she draws a thoughtful picture, he/she gets a chip.

He/she must respond to a **You Can't Make Me Do It!** situation (p. 26). The first time a circle is landed on, read the statement on the top of the page. Then the player should throw the 30-sided die to choose the situation. If he/she answers with a thoughtful response, he/she gets a chip.

The first time a player lands on a diamond, read the statement at the top of the **Keep It Steady** page. Each player landing on a diamond has 30 seconds to build a house of cards with the six **In Control** cards while the player on his/her right tries to distract him/her. The original player gets one chip for every card that is standing when the time is up, and an additional three bonus chips if he/she has shown absolutely no response to the distracting player.

The Star and Circle situations have five blank numbers for you to fill in by yourself or with the child. If you do not wish to add numbers 26 through 30, when these numbers come up on the die, the player should roll again.

Play proceeds until the first player lands back at the START. The player with the most chips at the end of the game is the winner.

Look Ahead!

WHEN THE FIRST STAR IS LANDED ON, READ THE FOLLOWING TO THE PLAYERS:

The following statements describe situations where you could get into trouble. In 60 seconds, draw a picture of a bad thing that could happen next.

★1. A kid you know wants you to go into the drugstore and steal some candy.

★2. Your friend sees that the ticket-taker at the movies has stepped away from the door. She says, "Why pay? Let's just sneak in!"

★3. You walk by the teacher's desk and see the answers to the quiz you are going to take that afternoon. If you look at it for just a minute, you could get the answers to the first five questions!

★4. You're playing catch and the ball rolls into the street. You don't see any cars coming, but you haven't really looked very hard.

★5. There is a long line at the water fountain, but all the kids in line are younger than you. You're really thirsty, so why not just butt in?

★6. You want money for the arcade after school. Just before you leave to go to the bus stop, you see your mom's wallet on the kitchen table.

★7. An older kid dares you to smoke a cigarette.

★8. A sign near the train tracks reads "DANGER! DO NOT CROSS TRACKS!", but your Frisbee just landed on the other side of those tracks.

★9. Your best friend is a math whiz. She tells you to sit behind her during the math test so you can copy her answers if you need to.

★10. The doors and windows to a newly-constructed house haven't been installed yet, and you see some lumber laying on the floor that would be perfect for a treehouse.

★11. You're trying to fix your bike when you see some tools your dad brought home from work.

★12. A man in a car pulls up alongside you as you're walking home and asks you for directions to the pizza parlor.

★13. One of the older boys brings some beer to your friend's party and asks if you want one. Your friend's parents are upstairs.

★14. You're walking home from the bus stop when a man approaches you and asks you if you want to get high.

★15. You don't know it, but your dad knows you cheated on your English test, because you got an "A" when you usually get "C"s. He asks you about it.

★16. Your mom has been nagging at you all afternoon to start your term paper and you've had it. You yell back at her, "LEAVE ME ALONE!"

★17. There's a new video game you're dying to have, but your parents say it's too expensive. As you're browsing around the video game section, you notice that all of the salespeople are busy with other customers.

★18. Your little sister tells your dad that you swear all the time.

★19. Some kids in your class have been teasing you ever since you started wearing glasses. One day they get on your nerves so much that you throw a punch at one of them, and the teacher sees it.

★20. You don't think you can handle your parents' constant fighting anymore, so you decide to run away. You wait until nighttime, pack your backpack, and set out for a friend's house.

★21. You know you're not allowed to play in your mom's study, but she has a great game on her computer that you want to try. While you're in there, you knock her favorite mug off her desk and it breaks.

★22. You have a hard time sitting still in class. Your teacher told you that if you get out of your seat one more time, you'll get detention.

★23. A dog is leashed to a tree, and its owner is working in the garden nearby. Your friend dares you to pull the dog's tail.

★24. You told your friend that your dad hides porno magazines in his drawer. When your friend comes over one day, he wants you to get them out so you can look at them.

★25. There's a girl in your class who you think you like. To get her attention, you hide her lunch, hoping she'll find out it was you who did it. Instead, she tells the teacher.

★26. _____

★27. _____

★28. _____

★29. _____

★30. _____

You Can't Make Me Do It!

WHEN THE FIRST CIRCLE IS LANDED ON, READ THE FOLLOWING TO THE PLAYERS:

Sometimes other people or certain situations can lead kids into trouble. Can you think of a situation where a person might make these statements to lead you, or someone else, into trouble? Describe the situation and tell what you would do.

●1.   "Come on, nobody's looking."

●2.   "Let's just do it once, okay?"

●3.   "I dare you to try it."

●4.   "Don't be a scaredy cat..."

●5.   "Quick...do it!"

●6.   "I bet you're afraid."

●7.   "What are you, chicken?"

●8.   "Let's go in and look around."

●9.   "Nothing will happen."

●10.   "Do it or you're out."

●11.   "All the other kids are doing it."

●12.   "You're not brave enough."

●13.   "You probably don't know how."

●14.   "Let's see if he can handle it."

●15. "You'd better...or else!"

●16. "If I can do it, you can too."

●17. "Come on, it's easy"

●18. "That's all it takes."

●19. "Go ahead...make my day."

●20. "You're with me, right?"

●21. "It's your turn."

●22. "I bet you can do that."

●23. "Run!"

●24. "Go for it."

●25. "You try it first."

●26. _____

●27. _____

●28. _____

●29. _____

●30. _____

Keep it Steady

WHEN THE FIRST DIAMOND IS LANDED ON, READ THE FOLLOWING TO THE PLAYERS:

Sometimes kids get angry or lose control when other kids tease or annoy them. If you can learn to ignore these kids, without losing your temper, then you will be making great progress at being IN CONTROL.

When you land on a DIAMOND, you must practice not letting other people get to you. Try to build a card house with the six IN CONTROL cards in this kit. Try to get them to stand up by leaning them against each other, as if you were building a house.

Meanwhile the player on your right gets to annoy you as much as possible! He/she can say or do anything, but cannot touch you or actually try to knock the cards over. You get one chip for every card you can keep standing after 30 seconds of being annoyed. If you can completely ignore the annoying person – not showing a single sign that he/she is bothering you – then you get a three-chip bonus.

IN CONTROL

IN CONTROL

IN CONTROL

IN CONTROL

IN CONTROL

IN CONTROL

SELF-COACHING

Introduction:

Many children with problem in self-control do not seem to think before they act. Research has suggested that these children have a developmental immaturity, and have not developed the use of inner speech for self-regulation and problem solving. Other children with problems in self-control may be very negative in their thinking, and say things to themselves that are not motivating or are self-defeating.

Training children to change the way they think takes time, and research suggests that while children can learn to think differently in the therapist's office, they do not typically transfer these new skills into the classroom or home. To be useful and effective, these new skills must be practiced and rewarded in the child's day-to-day situations.

Objectives:

- To teach children to say encouraging self-statements that will help them concentrate and work harder

- To teach children to turn negative self-statements into positive ones

- To teach children to use a five-step problem-solving process

What You Will Need:
1 pawn for each player
1 regular 6-sided die
1 30-sided die
Chips

Make copies of the following pages or remove them from this book:
Coaching Questions (p. 34)
Negative Thinking Statements (p. 38)

How to Play:

This game can be played by two to six players. The youngest player goes first and play proceeds in a clockwise direction. Each player rolls the die and moves his/her pawn the corresponding number of squares. If the player lands on a:

He/she must answer a **Coaching** question (p. 34). First read the statement at the top of the page, and then throw the 30-sided die to choose the question. If the player responds with a thoughtful coaching response, he/she gets one chip.

He/she must change a **Negative Thinking** statement into a positive one (p. 38). First read the statement at the top of the page, and then throw the 30-sided die to choose the statement that must be changed. If the player successfully changes the negative statement into a positive one, he/she gets one chip.

He/she must describe a current problem and use a five-step problem-solving process to come up with the best solution possible. The five steps of problem-solving are:

1. State the problem clearly.

2. Brainstorm different possible solutions.

3. Compare the different alternatives.

4. Decide on the best solution.

5. Consider what the results will be and make appropriate adjustments, if necessary.

If the player completes the five-step problem-solving process, he/she gets two chips.

Each list of questions has five blank numbers for you to fill in by yourself or with the child. If you do not wish to add numbers 26 through 30, when these numbers come up on the die, the player should roll again.

Play proceeds until the first player lands back at the START. The player with the most chips at the end of the game is the winner.

READ THE FOLLOWING STATEMENT ALOUD BEFORE YOU PLAY THE GAME:

Do you play any sports? Do you have a coach who tells you to concentrate a little harder or keep your eye on the ball? That's a coach's job – to help you improve your performance by giving you ways to correct problems and improve your skills. Your coach's job is to help you stay in control of your body and perform the best that you can.

Did you know that really good athletes become their own coaches, too? When they are trying to hit a ball, or jump farther, or run faster, they talk to themselves. They become "self-coaches," saying things that will help them concentrate, perform better, and stay in control.

You can become a self-coach, too. Talking to yourself can help you concentrate, work harder and longer, deal with problems, and even feel better about yourself!

Coaching

WHEN THE FIRST STAR IS LANDED ON, READ THE FOLLOWING TO THE PLAYERS:

There are many times when being your own coach and talking to yourself can help you solve problems and keep IN CONTROL. Read the following examples and then try to come up with your own self-coaching statements.

Examples:

A. James hated studying for spelling tests, but he knew that if he didn't study he would get a poor grade. What could he say to himself to help motivate him to study? A good answer might be: "If I really study hard, I will get a good grade and Mom and Dad will be proud of me. It's worth the effort."

B. Tyrone felt that because he was short he would never be a great basketball player. But he really liked to play. What could he say to himself that would help him keep trying? A good answer might be: "There are a lot of good but small basketball players. I'll work on 'outside' shots and get really good. Besides, enjoying basketball is the most important thing!"

★1.   Brenda had to take medicine every day to help her concentrate and pay attention. But she was embarrassed about it, and didn't want her teacher or parents to talk about it. What could Brenda say to herself to help her with this problem?

★2.   Gary was always getting teased, even though he didn't know why. The bigger kids kept on picking on him. What could Gary say to himself that would help him deal better with the teasing?

★3.   Chris had a really bad temper. His father said that he was like a stick of dynamite, always ready to explode. What could Chris say to himself to help him control his temper?

★4.   Vince was always late getting into his seat when class was supposed to start. His teacher thought that he was being uncooperative, but Vince just seemed to forget. What could Vince say to himself that would help him remember that being in his seat on time was important?

★5.   Shandra used to get into trouble because she took things that belonged to other children. She didn't really mean to be a thief, but she just took things anyway. What could Shandra say to herself that would help her remember not to take things?

★6.   Robin, Jessie, and Samantha were best friends. They did everything together. Then Robin began to spend more time with Samantha, and Jessie felt left out. What could Jessie say to herself to feel better?

★7.   Billy studied really hard for the math test, but he got a "C" anyway. Most of the other kids didn't do well either, but that didn't make him feel much better. What could he say to himself that would motivate him to keep trying his best?

★8.   Harry worked hard on his science project, but when he was about to turn it in, he realized he forgot to include a really important part. Now it was too late. What could Harry say to himself that would make him feel that he still did a good job?

★9.   It was Kate's turn to bring the jump rope. When the other kids saw her rope, they started teasing her because it was old and looked like it would break. Everyone else had new ones, but Kate needed more allowance money to buy a new one herself. What could she do to make herself feel good about bringing the jump rope?

★10. Andy and his best friend Adam were trading sports cards. Andy made a bad trade, and when he realized it, he asked Adam to give the card back. Adam said, "No way. You made the trade. You have to live with it." What could Andy say to himself that would make him feel better about his mistake?

★11. Fern liked hanging out with the cool kids, and she didn't want them to know that she was an honors student. But they found out and decided to dump her. What could Fern say to herself to feel proud of herself anyway?

★12. Lateesha had a $10 bill in her jewelry box. Mary was playing at Lateesha's one day, and asked if she could try on Lateesha's jewelry. When Mary left, the $10 bill was missing. What could Lateesha tell herself instead of confronting Mary?

★13. Mike liked to be the class clown. Whenever he'd do something funny, the kids would laugh at him, but he got in trouble with the teacher almost every time. What could Mike say to himself that would help him remember that being disruptive in class wasn't acceptable?

★14. Frankie was a good actress, and she always got the best parts in the school plays. She loved performing, but the way she acted made the other kids think she was stuck-up and a show-off. What could Frankie say to herself that would help her realize that sometimes being different is okay?

★15. Max's mom never let him go anywhere on his own. He wasn't even allowed to walk down the street to Alex's house by himself. He felt like she was treating him like a baby. What could Max say to himself that would help him deal with this problem?

★16. Tarique's parents just got divorced, and they both yell at him a lot. He wants to help, but doesn't know what to do. Lately, he's been thinking that they wouldn't have gotten divorced if he'd behaved better. What could Tarique say to himself to help him remember that divorce is never any one person's fault?

★17. Jenny's parents forced her to take piano lessons even though she hated practicing and playing the piano. "We didn't buy that piano for nothing!" they told her. What could Jenny say to herself to see some benefit of playing the piano?

★18. Larry's mom told him that he'd have to take the late bus home if he wanted to stay for after-school sports. "I can't pick you up because I have to work," she told him. The late bus dropped him off really far from home, and his book bag was so heavy. What could Larry say to himself to make the long walk easier?

★19. Owen really wanted that cool watch he saw at the store, so he did some odd jobs and earned enough money to buy it. When the kids at school saw him wearing it, they accused him of stealing it. No one believed that he bought it himself. "You could never make enough money to buy that," they said. What could Owen say to himself to remember that he didn't do anything wrong in this situation?

★20. Barbara was at a party where the other kids were smoking cigarettes. When Barbara went outside to get some fresh air, a kid offered her a cigarette. "No, thanks. I don't smoke," she said. When she went back into the house, everyone was staring at her and making fun of her. What could Barbara say to herself to remember that she is right?

★21. Pedro's dad died six months ago, and he still feels bad about it. He sees kids with their parents at the park, at the mall, everywhere. "They are so lucky," he thinks. What can Pedro say to himself to help feel better?

★22. Missy's parents can't afford to by her a computer, so she has to stay after school to use the one in the computer lab to do her homework. She feels bad because she thinks everyone feels sorry for her. What can Missy say to herself to remember the things she does have?

★23. Kyle has lots of friends, but on the first day of school, he finds he doesn't know anyone in his new class. What can Kyle say to himself to make the situation better?

★24. Maria has a terrible singing voice, and she knows it. The chorus teacher gives her a solo part, and she's terrified. She lets the teacher know how she feels, but the teacher says she has to try it. What can Maria tell herself to get through her ordeal?

★25. Glen is really good at Ping-Pong, but in the tournament, he loses in the first round. What can Glen say to himself to feel better?

★26. _____

★27. _____

★28. _____

★29. _____

★30. _____

Negative Thinking

WHEN THE FIRST CIRCLE IS LANDED ON, READ THE FOLLOWING TO THE PLAYERS:

Being negative can make bad things even worse, but positive thinking can often make things better. Change the following negative thoughts into positive ones.

Example:

Negative:	I can't do math.
Positive:	I can do better if I work at it.

Negative:	No one likes me.
Positive:	I can make new friends if I try.

●1. I hate homework.

●2. My parents make me go to bed too early.

●3. Everyone except me has the new video game.

●4. Nobody has the kinds of problems I have.

●5. I hate being a kid.

●6. I have to come home so early.

●7. School is hard.

●8. My parents are so tough on me.

●9. I have no one to play with.

●10. I'm bored.

●11. I'm not smart enough.

●12. Everyone else has cool clothes.

●13. My parents always tell me what to do.

●14. I hate my sister.

●15. I'm too fat.

●16. No one else's parents make them do chores.

●17. I never get to watch the TV shows I want to watch.

●18. I'll never have my own room.

●19. The older kids tease me all the time.

●20. I get left out of everything.

●21. I never get picked to be team captain.

●22. I'm too short.

●23. The older kids get to do everything.

●24. Why can't I ever go first?

●25   Everyone talks about me behind my back.

●26. _____

●27. _____

●28 _____

●29. _____

●30. _____

Game #4

RIGHT ON TIME!

===

Introduction:
Children with problems in self-control typically have problems in organizational skills as well. As compared to other children of the same age, they may have problems in attending to time, prioritizing their activities, and organizing themselves for academic or other tasks. This game is designed to teach children the importance of making a schedule and sticking to it.

Objectives:
- To help children learn to make a schedule of things they should do each day

- To help children learn the value of being organized, developing study skills, being in the right place at the right time, and so on

- To reward children for being on time

What You Will Need:
    1 regular 6-sided die
    1 30-sided die
    1 pawn
    Chips
    I.O.U. Cards (p. 51)

Make copies of the following pages, or remove them from the book:
    On Time Questions (p. 42)
    Daily Activities List (p. 44)
    Rewards (p. 46)
    Daily Activity Sheet (pp. 48-49)

How to Play:
This game is played differently from the other games in this book, and differently from other board games. It is not just a game, but actually part of a behavioral program designed to monitor a child's daily activities and reward tasks that are completed on time. The child with self-control problems is the only player. He/she plays the game once a day, for just 10 to 15 minutes, as a way of reviewing and monitoring a daily schedule. The game is played with the supervision of an adult (usually the parent) who is regularly with the child at the end of the day. Playing the game immediately after dinner is the best way to make sure that it is done consistently.

Before playing the game, the adult must complete the **Daily Activity Sheet** with the child. The sheet is designed to identify times and activities that are important to the child. The form should be as complete as possible before the game is played Note that it actually begins on the night before and ends at dinner time.

On the first day of the game, the adult should explain to the child the importance of being organized, planning ahead, and keeping to a schedule. The adult should explain that the game will be played every day for 10 to 15 minutes to review how successful the child has been at sticking to a schedule. With the filled-in daily schedule next to the game board, the child should roll the regular die and move his/her pawn the appropriate number of squares. When the player lands on a:

The player must answer an **On Time** question, by rolling the 30-sided die and answering the appropriate question. The player gets one chip for answering each question.

The player must check his/her **Daily Activities List** by rolling the 30-sided die and checking his/her schedule according to the numbered statement. The player gets three chips if he/she has completed that activity.

If the player gets five chips during 10 to 15 minutes of play, he/she rolls the 30-sided die for a **Reward** (p. 46). Use **I.O.U.** cards (p. 51) if the reward is not immediately available. Chips cannot be carried over to the next day.

Each list has five blank numbers for you to fill in by yourself or with the child. If you do not wish to add numbers 26 through 30, when these numbers come up on the die, the player should roll again.

Play proceeds for approximately 10 to 15 minutes, until the player lands back at the START.

On Time

★1. How does your mom feel when you are late for dinner?

★2. What does your mom say when you are late for dinner?

★3. Why do some people use an alarm clock in the morning?

★4. Why does the school bus come to your stop at a specific time each morning?

★5. What does your teacher do to help kids keep to a schedule each day?

★6. Do you know how much time it takes you to get dressed and ready on a school morning?

★7. Name at least three things you need to do in the bathroom before you can have breakfast.

★8. How would you get to school if you missed the bus in the morning?

★9. How would you get home if you missed the bus in the afternoon?

★10. What would happen if you did not come in from recess when the whistle blew (or the bell rang)?

★11. Why does the newspaper list the times that movies begin?

★12. How does your mom or dad help you to keep on a schedule at home?

★13. Does your mom or dad use a timer in the kitchen? What does he/she time with it?

★14 What would happen if your mom or dad came home late and nobody made dinner?

★15. What would happen if your dad put a cake in the oven and forgot to check how long it needed to be baked?

★16. What are some of the advantages to arriving at school early?

★17. What does your teacher do if schoolwork is turned in late?

★18. How do you know which TV programs are on at different times?

★19. What happens if you return library books late?

★20. How do passengers know when a train is coming to their stop?

★21. Why is it important to be on time for dinner?

★22. What would happen if your mother didn't pick you up at the movies when she said she would?

★23. What would happen if a kid didn't have any bedtime at all?

★24. What happens if you are late for school?

★25. What time do you leave your house for school?

★26. _____

★27. _____

★28. _____

★29. _____

★30. _____

Daily Activities List

Give yourself three chips if:

●1.   You got yourself dressed on time.

●2.   You brushed your teeth and combed your hair without a reminder.

●3.   You came in from recess when you were supposed to.

●4.   You wrote down your homework assignment in your notebook or plan book.

●5.   You wrote down your homework assignment before the teacher erased it from the board.

●6.   You checked the daily schedule in your classroom at least once during the day.

●7.   You came to breakfast on time.

●8.   You came to dinner on time.

●9.   You came to dinner with your hands washed.

●10.   You came inside from playing before dark.

●11.   You had the right materials at school today (e.g., sneakers on gym day, pens and pencils, and any special items needed).

●12.   You remembered your lunch or lunch ticket today.

●13.   You put your jacket and book bag away and got ready for work without a reminder.

●14.   You turned off the TV when you were asked.

●15. You turned off your bedroom lights when asked.

●16. You got into your seat after recess.

●17. You worked on a long-term project or read part of a book today.

●18. You got your book bag organized for tomorrow.

●19. You hung up your clothes and put away your toys after using them.

●20. You took a bath or shower as soon as you were asked to.

●21. You did your homework on time.

●22. You were on time for the school bus.

●23. You went to bed without a fuss.

●24. You did your chores exactly on time.

●25. You played this game on time.

●26. _____

●27. _____

●28. _____

●29. _____

●30. _____

◆

Rewards

◆1. Cookie

◆2 Extra half-hour of TV

◆3. Time with parent

◆4. Special meal

◆5. Trip to the zoo

◆6. 50 cents

◆7. Extra time on computer

◆8. Extra time on video games

◆9. Rent a video

◆10. Ice cream cone

◆11. Trip to a video arcade

◆12. Trip to miniature golf course

◆13. Pizza for dinner

◆14. Comic book

◆15. Subtract a chore

◆16. Bake cookies with a parent

◆17. New markers or crayons

◆18. Play a sport with a parent (basketball, bowling, etc.)

◆19. Parent reads a story

◆20. Make your own sundae

◆21. Donut

◆22. Trading cards (football, baseball, etc.)

◆23. Stay up a half-hour later

◆24. Kid's magazine

◆25. Paperback book

◆26. _____

◆27. _____

◆28. _____

◆29. _____

◆30. _____

Daily Activity Sheet

Child's Name _____

Day _____

Date _____

Adult Playing The RIGHT ON TIME! Game_____

	Activity	Done On Time	Partially Done	Not Done
Yesterday Evening				
6:30 pm				
7:00 pm				
7:30 pm				
8:00 pm				
8:30 pm				
9:00 pm				
9:30 pm				
10:00 pm				
10:30 pm				
11:00 pm				
Today				
6:00 am				
6:30 am				
7:00 am				
7:30 am				
8:00 am				

	Activity	Done On Time	Partially Done	Not Done
8:30 am				
9:00 am				
9:30 am				
10:00 am				
10:30 am				
11:00 am				
11:30 am				
12:00 noon				
12:30 pm				
1:00 pm				
1:30 pm				
2:00 pm				
2:30 pm				
3:00 pm				
3:30 pm				
4:00 pm				
4:30 pm				
5:00 pm				
5:30 pm				
6:00 pm				

Dear _____

I Owe You _____
_____
For Getting Points on the
"On-Time Game"

Signed _____
Date _____

Dear _____

I Owe You _____
_____
For Getting Points on the
"On-Time Game"

Signed _____
Date _____

Dear _____

I Owe You _____
_____
For Getting Points on the
"On-Time Game"

Signed _____
Date _____

Dear _____

I Owe You _____
_____
For Getting Points on the
"On-Time Game"

Signed _____
Date _____

Dear _____

I Owe You _____
_____
For Getting Points on the
"On-Time Game"

Signed _____
Date _____

Dear _____

I Owe You _____
_____
For Getting Points on the
"On-Time Game"

Signed _____
Date _____

Game #5

HELPING OTHERS

Introduction:
Children with problems in self-control are frequently described as difficult and disruptive. A great deal of attention is focused on their problem behaviors, and so naturally they begin to incorporate these messages into their self-concepts. For this reason, it is important to not just prevent children from being bad, but to also teach them to be good. This game is intended to teach and reinforce the values of altruism and selflessness.

Objectives:
- To teach children the value of helping others

- To make random acts of kindness a part of every day

- To recognize when others are in need of help

What You Will Need:
1 pawn for each player
1 regular 6-sided die
1 30-sided die
Chips

Make copies of the following pages or remove them from the book:
Being Considerate Questions (p. 55)
Random Acts of Kindness Questions (p. 57)
Helper Questions (p. 59)

How to Play:

This game can be played by two to six players. The youngest player goes first and play proceeds in a clockwise direction. Each player rolls the die and moves his/her pawn the corresponding number of squares. If the player lands on a:

The player must answer a **Being Considerate** question by rolling the 30-sided die and answering the appropriate numbered question. The player gets one chip for answering each question.

The player must answer a **Random Acts of Kindness** question by rolling the 30-sided die and answering the appropriate numbered question. The player gets one chip for answering each question.

The player must answer a **Helper** question by rolling the 30-sided die and answering the appropriate numbered question. The player gets one chip for answering each question.

Each list includes five blank numbers for you to fill in by yourself or with the child. If you do not wish to add numbers 26 through 30, when these numbers come up on the die, the player should roll again.

Play proceeds until the first player lands back at the START. The player with the most chips at the end of the game is the winner.

Being Considerate

Give one chip for a good answer.

★1.   In what month do we celebrate Mother's Day?

★2.   When is your father's birthday?

★3.   Who will you buy presents for during Christmas or Hanukkah?

★4.   What could you do for your mom's birthday if you didn't have any money?

★5.   On what occasions or holidays do people often send cards? Name at least three.

★6.   Why do parents often buy teachers presents at the end of the school year?

★7   If you wanted to make a birthday card, what materials would you need?

★8.   Say at least three polite expressions.

★9.   If your friend lost his jacket, what could you say or do to help?

★10. If your friend looked very sad, what could you say or do to help?

★11. If a new kid in your class was alone on the playground, what could you do to make him feel like he fit in?

★12. Why do we have a day called "Teacher Appreciation Day" each spring?

★13. When you visit with an older relative (perhaps your grandmother or grandfather) how do you act differently than at other times? Why?

★14 When your mom or dad comes home from grocery shopping, what can you do to help?

★15. If your mom or dad has a headache, what can you do to help?

★16. When dinner is finished, what can you do that would be considerate?

★17. If your mom were on a diet, what could you do differently at home?

★18. If you came home from baseball practice full of mud, what could you do that would be considerate?

★19. If someone in your class broke his/her leg and wore a cast, name at least three things you could do to help.

★20. Pretend you are answering the phone. What do you say?

★21. When is your mother's birthday?

★22. How do you think your father would feel if you forgot all about Father's Day?

★23. Why do people write thank-you notes?

★24. Why would someone get mad if you showed up late for his/her party?

★25. Do you think a teacher cares if you hand in your work late?

★26. _____

★27. _____

★28. _____

★29. _____

★30. _____

●

Random Acts of Kindness

READ ALOUD WHEN A PLAYER LANDS ON A CIRCLE FOR THE FIRST TIME:

One of the best ways to make the world a better place is to treat everyone in it a little better. Many people, both adults and kids, make the world a better place by doing something nice for someone else every day. It only takes a minute to be thoughtful and considerate of someone else.

● 1. Name someone who likes to get a phone call from you.

● 2. Say something nice to the person sitting next to you.

● 3. Talk about the best present you ever gave someone and why it was good.

● 4. Think of an extra chore you can do today at home.

● 5   Think of something you can tell your teacher that he/she will like hearing.

● 6. Name a chore you could help your dad do today.

● 7. Name something that you could do that would really please your mom.

● 8. What could you do to let someone know that you want to be his or her friend?

● 9. What would be the best thing you could do to help your brother?

● 10 Tell about how you feel about learning to do a new chore that would make things easier for your parents (like laundry, unloading the dishwasher, etc.).

● 11. How do you think your neighbor would feel if you offered to take his or her dog for a walk?

● 12. Tell how you would thank your dad for something he does for you.

● 13. What could you do to make your teacher chuckle (that wouldn't get you into trouble)?

14. Tell about a time you helped a friend with a tough decision. What did you do?

15. Tell about a time when you did something for someone without being asked.

16. What would you plan for a secret celebration (even if it's a small one) for a loved one's birthday?

17. Convince the person on your right that using drugs is a bad idea.

18. Tell what you would say when your mom asks you to do something that needs to be done immediately (even if you're busy).

19. Think of someone you're angry with. What are three things you could say to make things better?

20. Let the person on your left take your next turn.

21 What would you do if there was just one more ketchup packet and you and your friend both needed it for hamburgers?

22. What is something special you could do for your mom on a weekend morning?

23. Tell why it is sometimes helpful to just listen to a person talk about his or her problems, even though it doesn't seem like you're doing anything to help.

24. What is a gift you could give your dad for his birthday that he would really appreciate?

25. How could you let your little sister know that you care about her (even though sometimes it seems like you're her enemy)?

26. _____

27. _____

28. _____

29. _____

30. _____

Helper

◆1. What would you do if you saw a baby left alone in a stroller, and no one else was around?

◆2. What would you do or say if your mother said, "I don't feel well. I'm going to lie down"?

◆3. What would you do if you saw a very old person standing on the corner, looking confused?

◆4. How do you know if someone needs help, even though the person insists that he/she doesn't need it?

◆5. Name a charity or organization that helps other people.

◆6. How could someone who knows his way around the neighborhood help a new kid on the block?

◆7. How could you help someone who you saw fall and hurt himself or herself?

◆8. Is it a good idea to help a stranger who asks you for help? Why or why not?

◆9. How can you help someone who seems sad?

◆10. Why do you think people go to their clergy (priest, minister, rabbi) for help?

◆11. Should you help a kid who "cries wolf" all the time?

◆12. How can you help to make your neighborhood safer?

◆13. What can you do to clean up your street?

◆14. What does a charity do? Is there a charity group you would like to join? What is it?

◆15. What could you do to help a kid who is sad because he/she wasn't chosen for either kickball team at recess?

◆16. Ask the player of your choice to tell you something that you could do to help him/her.

◆17. What would you do if you were talking to a friend on the phone, and your mom called you for help?

◆18. How could you help someone bake a cake if you had no idea how to do it?

◆19. Name three things you could do to your room that would help your mom.

◆20. Name three things that people lose often. How could you help find them?

◆21. Tell how you would be helping someone by refusing to fight with him/her.

◆22. How could you help someone who didn't have enough money to buy his/her lunch?

◆23. Why would it be considered helpful if you agreed to do an activity with a friend, even though you didn't really want to do it?

◆24. Tell why it is helpful to follow the rules in your family.

◆25. Give an example of when it would be helpful to donate some of your time to a good cause.

◆26. _____

◆27. _____

◆28. _____

◆29. _____

◆30. _____

CAN I PLAY, TOO?

Introduction:
Children with problems in self-control often have problems with their peers. They may have trouble controlling their tempers, may be overly impulsive in their play and not follow rules, may not respect the rights or feelings of others, and so on. As a result, these children may have few friends and be isolated and lonely. Sometimes when problems are extreme, they may be rejected by their peer group and teased. Alternatively, these children can gravitate towards other children who have poor impulse control and engage in inappropriate, dangerous, or even delinquent behaviors.

The game format is a particularly effective way to teach social skills to children, because it presents a structured environment in which children relate to each other by following rules.

Objectives:
- To teach children how to engage other children in play or other activities
- To teach children how to develop a best friend
- To teach children how to cooperate in group activities

What You Will Need:
> 1 pawn for each player
> 1 regular 6-sided die
> 1 30-sided die
> Chips

Make copies of the following pages or remove them from the book:
> **I Want To Play** Questions (p. 63)
> **Best Friend** Questions (p. 66)
> **Friends' Club** Questions (p. 68)

How to Play:

The game can be played by two to six players. The youngest player goes first and play proceeds in a clockwise direction. Each player rolls the 6-sided die and moves his/her pawn the corresponding number of squares. If the player lands on a:

The player must answer an **I Want To Play** question by rolling the 30-sided die and answering the appropriate numbered question. The player gets one chip for answering each question.

The player must answer a **Best Friend** question by rolling the 30-sided die and answering the appropriate numbered question. The player gets one chip for answering each question.

The player must answer a **Friend's Club** question by rolling the 30-sided die and answering the appropriate numbered question. The player gets one chip for answering each question.

Each list of questions includes five blank numbers for you to fill in by yourself or with the child. If you do not wish to add numbers 26 through 30, when these numbers come up on the die, the player should roll again.

Since the game is designed to promote social interaction, it should not have an individual winner. All players win when at least 25 chips have been accumulated and pooled together. When this happens, the players should choose a group activity as a reward, such as seeing a movie together, sharing a treat, etc.

I Want to Play

Players get one chip for a good answer.

★1   What would you do if you wanted to play soccer with a group of kids but they said that you weren't good enough?

★2.   If you wanted to ask someone to come to your house next Saturday afternoon, what would you do?

★3.   Turn to the person on your right and try to guess his/her favorite TV show.

★4.   Turn to the person on your left and try to guess his/her favorite board game.

★5.   What would you do if someone called you a cheater?

★6.   What would you do if you knew that someone else was cheating at a game?

★7.   What would you do if you were playing baseball, and someone deliberately tripped you as you were running the bases?

★8.   Name two really good friends from a movie or TV show.

★9.   Who could you talk to if you feel that nobody likes you? What would you say?

★10.   Tell the person on your left something that he/she doesn't know about you.

★11.   What would you do if you accidentally sat in someone's chair, and he/she was angry about it?

★12.   Tell about a time when you shared something with someone you didn't know very well. What was the outcome?

★13.   Pretend the person across from you is the most popular kid in the class, and you're new to the school. How would you introduce yourself?

★14. You like the kid who lives next door, but your best friend doesn't. Should you play with the kid next door or not? Why?

★15 Do you think it's fair to exclude players from competitive teams because they aren't good enough?

★16. If you had a friend at your house, and another friend called to play with you, would you include him/her or say that you were already playing with someone?

★17. How would someone feel if you told him/her that you didn't want to play? Why is it sometimes nicer not to be totally honest?

★18. Do you always have to like someone immediately to spend time with him/her? Why or why not?

★19. How would you approach a group of kids who look like they are having a great time together?

★20. What would you do if everyone played jump rope at recess and you couldn't jump rope at all?

★21. If someone asked to borrow your ball to play soccer, but didn't ask you to play too, what would you do?

★22. What would you do if a kid you really like asked you to play, but you had tons of homework?

★23. What would you do if you were playing at the park and your friend said, "See those bikes over there? Let's borrow them for a while and take a ride!"?

★24. Ask the person on your right to tell you his or her favorite food, and tell yours.

★25. What could you say to someone who you don't know, but recognize from your math class?

★26. _____

★27. _____

★28. _____

★29. _____

★30. _____

●

Best Friend

Players get one chip for a good answer.

●1. What does your best friend look like? If you don't have a best friend, what do you think yours would look like?

●2. What would you get a best friend for a birthday present?

●3 What would you do if your best friend was mad at you because you were supposed to call, but you didn't?

●4. Would you care if your best friend looked different from most other people (for example, if he/she was of a different race, or handicapped)? Why or why not?

●5. What do you think your best friend would say his or her favorite movie is?

●6. What's the best thing about your best friend's personality?

●7. Name three things about your best friend that are very different from you.

●8. Why is your best friend the person you like most?

●9. What would you do if your best friend said something that hurt your feelings?

●10. What would you do if your best friend told someone your secret?

●11. Could you trust your best friend if he/she told someone something that was a secret?

●12. Name something about your best friend that you would change if you could.

●13. 1f you didn't like your best friend's mom, would you tell him/her? Why or why not?

●14. If your best friend wanted you to take drugs with him/her, what would you do?

●15. If you made a bet with your best friend and he lost, would you hold him to it?

●16. If your parents told you to do something, and your best friend thought you shouldn't do it, what would you do?

●17. What would you say to your best friend if you wanted to spend time with someone else (without him/her)?

●18. If you and your best friend wanted to sign up for a trip, but there was only one seat left on the bus, what would you do?

●19. Can you have two best friends? Why or why not?

●20. What's the difference between a best friend and a regular friend?

●21. What would be something you would do for a best friend if he/she were sick?

●22. What would you do if your parents didn't like your best friend?

●23. Was there one quality you found in your best friend that you didn't find in anyone else? What was it?

●24. How did your best friend get to be your best friend?

●25. What would you do if someone you didn't know very well introduced you to someone else as his/her best friend?

●26. _____

●27. _____

●28. _____

●29. _____

●30. _____

Friends' Club

Players get one chip for a good answer.

◆1. If you had a club, what would you name it?

◆2. If you had a club, who would you want to be in it?

◆3. Why is teamwork important in a sport?

◆4. What would you do if you were on a team, but the other kids never let you play?

◆5. Do you think that boys- or girls-only teams are a good idea?

◆6. If someone wanted to join your club, but you already had enough members, would you let him/her join anyway? Why or why not?

◆7. Is there anything you could do if you were always picked last for the team? What would it be?

◆8. Do you think that kids who are not talented in something should be included anyway? (For example, should kids who don't play chess well be on a chess team?)

◆9. Give an example of a game or sport that requires as many people as possible to be on each side.

◆10. Can a group or club decide to "own" or take over a piece of public property, like a jungle gym or tennis court? Why or why not?

◆11. If you were asked to join a club, would you join it even if your best friend wasn't included? Why or why not?

◆12. If you were a member of a club, what would you do if everyone was required to do something you didn't want to do?

◆13. Why do people tend to exclude someone who is not a "team player?"

◆14. What does "exclusive" mean? Should clubs be exclusive?

◆15. How is a class like a team? Give three examples.

◆16. Why is it important to follow the rules of a group? What would happen if nobody paid attention to the rules?

◆17. What would happen if all the players in a football game decided to choose their own positions while they were playing the game?

◆18. How do you think the other players would feel if you suddenly decided to stop playing this game? Why?

◆19. Name three things that a club could do to improve their neighborhood.

◆20. What would you do if the members of your group ganged up on you?

◆21. Why is it sometimes so hard for two different groups to get along?

◆22. Do you think groups should be racially mixed? Why or why not?

◆23. If you felt sad or angry, would you feel comfortable sharing your feelings with the whole group, or would you rather talk to just one person?

◆24. How are the people who work for a company like a team?

◆25. What is your favorite sports team? Why do you like that team?

◆26. _____

◆27._____

◆28. _____

◆29. _____

◆30. _____